Ocean Butterfly

A True Story of Surviving Domestic Violence

Carol Watson

ISBN: 978-1547274413

ISBN: 1547274417

Manufactured in the United States of
America

First Edition published 2017

Dedication

To my parents, who taught me well and raised me right.

Contents

Acknowledgements

First of all, I thank God for my talent and for allowing me to live my dream as an author. Thank you to all the teachers and professors who helped me with my writing during the early years. To my family and friends who were there for me during one of the worst times in my life, thank you for being there and for supporting me. I would also like to thank the counselors, friends, and the countless people in South Carolina who were there to help me along the way. Special thanks to Sandra Eason and Dorthea Knox for inspiring and encouraging me to write my story. I appreciate each and every one of you!

Author's note

This is a true story about an extremely painful time in my life. The events in this book are written from the best way that I can remember them. Some of my friends' names have been changed to protect their privacy. This has been the hardest book that I have written, but if it can help prevent someone from making a bad choice then it would be worth it. I am a domestic violence survivor, and my hope and my prayer is that my story will be an inspiration to others.

Blessings,

Carol Watson

The Caterpillar

I'm a lowly caterpillar,
Just crawling along.
Afraid to try, afraid to cry,
Only want to survive and to fly.

I had always wanted to be married. However, when I was married I hated it. Really really hated it! He would punch me, and then he would laugh at me when I told him it hurt.

I met Allan in June 1998. It was through some telephone dating service, but I do not remember what it was called. We arranged to meet at the Burger King in Mooresville, North Carolina. He lived in Catawba County and Mooresville was half way between where we lived.

When I first saw Allan, I thought he was the ugliest thing that I had ever laid eyes on. I wish I would have turned tail and ran, but I'm the type of person who likes to give everyone a chance. We spoke a few words and I was embarrassed because things were falling out of my car.

For our first date, we went to Concord to get something to eat and to hang out at a family fun center that had a racetrack. We rode go-carts. Somehow, that day I knew I would marry him.

We met up a few other times and later that summer, mom and I let him move in with us. After Allan had lived there for a few months, we found out mom had breast cancer. During that difficult time, I was so glad that he was there! He helped to give me the moral support that I needed, and later that fall we decided we wanted to get married.

I was so worried about what was going to happen to my mother that I did not realize that I was getting ready to make the biggest mistake of my life. Sometimes when a person is faced with something frightening and unknown, common sense totally goes out the window. I was not thinking straight because worry and fear got in the way. A close cousin informed me a few years later that that is exactly what had happened, only at the time I did not see it.

A few weeks before the wedding, I remembered feeling scared and thinking I did not really want to marry Allan, but I did not think I could back out of it then either. I had mistaken those feelings for the so-called nerves. I messed up and made a lot of mistakes along the way. I am so ashamed that I lied to everyone and to God, and I often wonder if He will ever be able to forgive me!

Allan and I got married on December 11th, 1998. It was a small and private ceremony at home with only family and close friends in attendance. I knew before the wedding that I did not love him the way I should. I went into the marriage thinking love would come later. I had always heard that love grows with time, and sometimes with some people that can be true, but just because you grow up hearing something your whole life does not always mean that it is true! In our marriage, the only things that grew were hate and resentment.

One of the reasons why I married Allan is because I felt sorry for him. His parents were killed in a car accident (not at the same time) when he was a small child, and his grandmother raised him. We had been led to believe that he did not have family, but we found out later that he had aunts, uncles, and cousins. They seemed like nice people when I met them and I had liked his aunt and uncle, his mother's brother and sister.

Another reason is because I felt even sorrier for myself. I had been picked on and made fun of a lot in my life and at the time I did not think that I could do any better. I had always wanted to find love, get married, and have children, but it had not happened for me. I had just turned 26 years old shortly before Allan and I met.

One of my best friends, who had attended my wedding, told me later that he knew my marriage would not last, but he could not tell me. I wish he would have spoken up, although it probably would not have changed anything. When I married Allan, I did not realize that he could be such a mean-spirited person. He had been nice when we met and I thought he really cared about me.

I had hoped we could learn to love each other and be good for one another, but obviously that did not happen. I never thought he could turn out to be someone that would hurt me so badly! We argued a lot and we didn't always get along before we got married, but I mistakenly thought it would get better. It doesn't. If there is a lot of arguing in a relationship before, it will only get worse after marriage. That was a hard lesson I had to learn.

Is it possible that my husband knew that I truly did not love him? I know in my heart that I tried to and really wanted to love him, but I feel as though I failed when I could not. I learned the hard way that you cannot make yourself love someone, any more than you can make them love you! One thing is for certain; no matter what went on or how miserable I became, I always remained faithful. I took my vows seriously and I just wanted things to be right in the marriage.

That's not to say that I was perfect by any means; I certainly wasn't. I did do wrong and I said a lot of things that I regret. Sometimes Allan made me so angry that I hit him too during our heated arguments, and one time I grabbed at his neck wanting to choke him! There were times when I looked into his eyes and told him that I hated him, and the sad thing was that at those moments it was the truth. It was only by the grace of God that we did not kill each other!

Allan was not only an abuser, but also a liar. He did a lot of sneaky things while we were married, but mom had ways of catching him in his lies. One evening, Allan brought home a Sony PlayStation that he claimed his best friend had given him. We thought that sounded fishy, but we soon forgot about it.

Sometime later, a man who had owned a service station in Cleveland called and wanted to know why Allan had not paid him for some work that he had done on his car. Mom had suspicions right away. Somehow she was able to get a phone number for Allan's best friend's brother, and he confirmed to her that his brother had not given Allan that game. By then, that supposed best friend had moved to Michigan.

Allan had used the money for car work to buy the game. He had denied that at first, but then he finally admitted it when mom and I took him to the man's garage to talk to him. Allan had said he did not owe the man money and he was trying to get out of paying him. Mom told Allan that his grandmother would not want him to do things like that and she would not be happy. His grandmother had passed away a few months before that.

After Allan lost his grandmother, he often did what he wanted to do and it was like nothing else mattered to him anymore. I was starting to see that he could not be trusted at all, and if you don't have trust in a marriage, you don't have anything. Another hard lesson learned, but wisdom gained.

In May 2000, we were in a car accident, which has left me with lasting back and neck problems. The realization that Allan really did not care about me, or what happened to me, came when I was at the hospital, scared and alone, while he was out doing other things. For a while after that, I was under chiropractor care and I went through some anxiety and depression.

Allan and I lived with mom until September 2000 when we moved to an apartment complex near the mall. We had used most of my settlement to move, but if I had known how things would be, I definitely would have done things differently! I had nearly changed my mind about moving there when I had heard a lot of bad things about it, but I had no say in the matter. With Allan, it always had to be his way or no way!

We started out in a small studio apartment that was actually kind of neat. It had a bed that pulled out of the wall and a space with mirrors and glass shelves to put things. Allan bought my first rabbit for me, a black and white Dutch, and I named it Scamper. I liked having our own place, but then after we were on our own for a while, things began to change. Allan had a very bad temper and one night he got up and beat on the cage when Scamper made noises.

A few weeks before Christmas, we had the option to move into a one bedroom apartment in another building. Thinking we would have more room and a nicer place, we agreed to the move. However, things were starting to go downhill in our marriage then.

Late one night, I was in the bathroom feeling very sick. I was crying and begging for Allan to help me. All he would do was fuss at me without coming to see if I needed anything and that made me feel even worse.

A few weeks later, we rented our first computer and that's when the problems escalated. When Allan was home, he stayed on it much of the time and he was always talking to other women. I did not like that a bit and we argued and fought constantly. Sometimes he would cuss me out. I'm sure our next door neighbor heard us. Our fights could get very loud. I worried about being reported to the landlord and thrown out.

One night, Allan and I got into an argument that became so intense that I ran out of the apartment and ran across Highway 70 to the gas station nearby. He later came looking for me in the car and I went back home with him. I did not want to go back. I was sick and tired of him having his way all the time about everything.

Allan hit me a few times, but the worst part was the verbal abuse. He always put me down and made me feel like I couldn't do anything right. I thought I wasn't good enough or pretty enough, but the truth is he wasn't good enough for me! Even before I found out what a rotten worm he really was, I wanted out and away from him. I resented him and the way he treated me.

Things got to the point where I was not allowed to cry around Allan. If I did, it was a cussing out for sure. He tried to control me and he would not let me work, even though I was willing. When he did work, I was stuck in that small apartment by myself. We only had one car and I could not go anywhere.

Allan could not seem to get along with other people and he would not keep a job. He was constantly bouncing from one place to another, yet he was always wasting money on things we did not need. One afternoon he went out and bought a bigger rabbit cage and two white baby bunnies. I thought this was unnecessary since we had Scamper, but I did not try to talk him out of it. He would not have listened to me anyway, so why start arguments when they could be avoided?

Scamper did not like the rabbits and he growled or hissed. That was something I'd never heard him do and we were concerned. Instead of setting the cages in separate rooms, Allan took my rabbit and let him loose in a small patch of woods off of highway 70. In my heart I really loathed him for that, but I was not allowed to cry about it. If I could have done it over, I would have kept my rabbit and let Allan go!

In the spring of 2001, after living in our house for over 26 years, mom had to move out due to circumstances that were beyond her control. She moved into a duplex on Hurley School Road. The two apartments were in a nice location beside each other and her cousin lived across the road.

When we found out that one of the apartments became available several weeks later, Allan and I moved into it. I really enjoyed living in the duplex and there was much more room. Mom was very close and I was constantly running across the yards to do laundry or to hang out with her. I was happy living there and things got better in my life for a little while. Allan and I were actually getting along. Although we had argued and fought much of the time, we did have our share of good times. He took me to several great rock concerts, including my first Kiss concert, and we even met a few of the band members from other bands.

I was excitedly awaiting my birthday in June. We had our tickets for the Poison concerts and things lined up in the fan clubs to possibly be able to meet the band. They would be in Charlotte the night after my birthday and in Raleigh the night after that, and I was super excited about getting to see them in concert two nights straight!

Poison has been my favorite rock band since I was sixteen years old. Contrary to what some ignorant people may think, it has absolutely nothing to do with worshipping them! Anyone who knows me well enough knows how much I love that band, their music, and going to see them in concert. They are the inspiration for the rock band in my novels. Part of the reason that I am alive is because of some of their songs. Many of them helped me to get through some of the worst times in my life! So for me, that runs much deeper than just being a fan!

That's not to say that God didn't bring me through those times ~ HE did! No matter what we go through in life, God always provides something to get us through the bad times, whether it is a song, another person, or something else. It has always been through Poison's music that I was able to survive some of the hardest things that I have ever been through, and I thank God for that band!

As always, the Poison concert in Charlotte on June 5th was fantastic! I was happy and thankful to be there, and after the show we had our passes to meet Rikki. He had his own fan club. I was so excited that I could hardly wait to meet him! I became even more excited when Lorna, one of our friends who we had met up with at the concert, told me that Bobby was there. At first I thought Lorna was kidding, but then I finally did see Bobby in the crowd and I could hardly believe it!

Meeting Bobby was seriously a major dream come true! He had always been my favorite in the band. He was very nice and a lot of fun to be around in person. I got his autograph and had my picture taken with him. The only regret I have is that Lorna is in the photo with us. She is not a friend anymore, and we have not talked to each other in years.

I do not remember what I said to Bobby, but I was one extremely happy and excited girl! We met Rikki briefly and then I ran back to Bobby and kissed him on the cheek. Yes, I really did that! ☺ He was cool about the whole thing and he picked with me. He was so cute and funny that I didn't want the moment to end! I was totally ecstatic and riding high after meeting those guys!

The concert in Raleigh the next night was even more exciting. We were on the third row from the stage, and again we had passes to see Rikki. I was also in Bret's fan club and I was looking forward to meeting him again. I had met him the year before at a concert there in Raleigh.

Before the concert was over, however; Allan ruined the night for me. He took my pass to meet Rikki and gave it to someone else, just because he did not think I could do both meet and greets! Then to make matters worse, he met Bret when he wasn't even in his fan club. Bret just happened to see Allan when he was walking around looking for me. I was so mad at Allan for cheating me out of my chance of meeting Rikki, and possibly Bobby again, that I was ready to wring his head off! He had done a lot of detestable things to me, but that was the meanest.

I did eventually meet Rikki again though when my sister took me to a Poison concert in June 2007. She was blessed with the chance to meet him too and he was so nice!

Even though it has been awhile, I still hope and pray that somehow, someway, that I may be able to meet Bobby again. Not only just to meet him, but to have something that was so spitefully taken away to be made up.

Being able to meet Bret, Rikki, and Bobby was a true blessing, and that has definitely been the best thing that has ever happened to me in my life! I really and truly thank God for letting it happen for me! There are no words to describe the gratefulness that I feel in my heart! It is something most of my relatives and friends could never possibly understand, unless they have experienced it for themselves. Having those memories and having that awesome experience would be what would help carry me through a dark, painful time that would soon follow.

On June 18th, one of the worst things that had ever happened to me happened. I found out that Allan had been cheating on me. A little over a week before that, he had let a girl come to stay with us, who he had claimed to be a long lost cousin from Texas. They had met online.

I knew right away what was up, but I did not know what to do about it, so I waited and let things play out. When Allan first told me about the girl, I knew it was a girlfriend. We had had many arguments the months before because of him talking to other women online. I do not blame the internet for what happened. I figure eventually it would have been someone else some other way. Allan was that type of person.

I do not remember the actual details of what went on that night, as so much of it is a blur, but I do remember feeling that things could not keep going on like they were. That day I had mostly sat around moping. It seems like Allan was out somewhere most of the day, work perhaps, but I really can't remember. My cousin Sabina came over because I needed someone to talk to and we went over to mom's apartment. It was there where all hell broke loose.

When Allan came in that evening, I asked him to tell me the truth about the girl, but he kept denying it. Some time or another, the girl had admitted to us that she was not his cousin and that she did not know he was married when she came here. He had lied to her too! I cannot even begin to imagine what she must have gone through! I do not know what ever happened to her, as I guess they took her away when the law was called out.

When Allan finally admitted that the girl was a girlfriend, I totally lost it! I started slapping him and hitting him for everything he wasn't worth! It took my mom and Sabina to physically pull me away from him. I'm sure I cussed him out plenty too. The shock I was in was too much for me and I had to be taken to hospital by ambulance.

I really thought my life was over that night! I was extremely sad, angry, and disappointed that my marriage had turned out like it had. I think a patient advocate talked to me some, but I really do not remember much about what went on at the hospital.

The next morning, I was at mom's apartment with her after being released, but I could not return home until a police officer could escort me over. This was for my own protection after the domestic dispute the night before. Allan was at home, but I was not allowed to go back to my own home after everything that I had been through, and I was absolutely livid! I had never felt so much anger and frustration over the unfairness of it all. I did my share of screaming, yelling, and crying; trying to fight my way back home!

Later, an officer did show up and take me home and he stayed with us while Allan packed his stuff to leave. He told me that he was sorry and he loved me, and he handed me a note. I read it, wadded it up, and threw it at him. I'm not sure what I did or said after that, but of course with the officer there I could not say what I really wanted to say!

After Allan left, I finally had time to myself to pick up the pieces and try to make sense out of all that had transpired. I was hurting so much emotionally that I just wanted to give up and end it all then! I felt so much despair that I was not sure that I could survive another hour, another minute, or even another second.

I put in a Poison CD and listened to the songs "Something to Believe In" and "Every Rose Has It's Thorn." I played them over and over, and I cried until I thought I might make it through that dark moment after all. I thank God for those songs and for the strength to get through that horrible day!

After some time, Allan called me. He said he loved me and that he could not live without me. Then he pretended to cry, but I did not fall for it. I was thinking, "Oh no you don't! Don't even try that with me!" I guess he really thought he would be able to get me back by pretending to care. I know that if he had ever really loved me at all, he never would have tried to move a girlfriend in with us! That phone call was the last time we ever had contact.

Later that afternoon, Sabina came to check on me and she took me to a place in town for counseling. It was through that that I learned of a shelter for women and children who had been abused. I never knew that such a place even existed. I agreed to go and arrangements were made for me to move into it that evening. One of the rules for staying there were that we were not allowed to have any contact at all with the person who had abused us. That was fine with me; I never wanted to see Allan again anyway!

The counselors who I met were very nice and they really helped me. They were there to talk to me when I needed it, and it was through one of them that I would make a decision that would change my life. It was also helpful interacting with other ladies who had been through some of the same things that I had been through. We were all there to help and support each other during a very dark time in our lives.

I did not stay at the shelter all day. Sometimes mom and I went out and did things, or Sabina would take me somewhere. One day she took me to one of mom's cousins to deliver my two rabbits. I could not keep them and he had said he would take them. His children had animals. I really hated giving my rabbits away, but I could not care for them at the shelter and I knew I would be moving out of the duplex soon.

One morning, I did something to get back at Allan. I withdrew most (if not all) of the money from our bank account. One of the managers at our bank had informed mom that the other branch in town opened half an hour earlier than the one we usually went to.

Early that morning, mom took me to the other bank and I took out the money, and when we drove by our bank, we saw the car in the lot. Allan was waiting for the bank to open so that he could get paid. His pay from work was set up to go into the account automatically and I'm sure he was mad as a hornet when he found out the money was not there! My, oh my, how I would have liked to have been a fly on that wall! We were a bit concerned, wondering if he may try to come by later and bother us, but he didn't. He was probably afraid to. After all of the lies that he had been caught in, he was afraid of mom and he often tried to hide from her. He was a coward and an idiot, among everything else.

During the two weeks that I stayed in the shelter, I made one of the most important decisions that I would ever make. I had found out that it was possible that I could be transferred to another shelter somewhere else if I wanted to be. After a few days, my counselor got back to me and told me that the shelter in Myrtle Beach would take me in, but I would have to leave the next day!

One of my biggest dreams had always been to live near the beach. I finally had a chance to do it and I was going to take it! The hardest part of all was breaking the news and saying goodbye to my aunts, uncles, and cousins. Mom and I spent all afternoon packing and doing all that I needed to do before I would leave.

Early the next morning, we got my ticket from the shelter. They paid the whole bus fare to transfer me to the shelter in Myrtle Beach! I did not have a car because Allan took it when he left. Mom took me to the Greyhound bus station and it was so hard saying goodbye to her! I would really miss her and everyone in my family, but I knew in my heart what I had to do.

If I had known how hard things would be I honestly don't know that I would have gone through with it. I wanted to move to the beach so badly that I had the determination to go! I would make things work out somehow! My exact thoughts at the time were just get me the hell out of Salisbury! I was tired of being afraid and worrying that Allan could be lurking somewhere. After all of the times that he had threatened me and people in my family, I did not feel safe living in my own home town anymore!

Ironically, it was through one of the most devastating things that had ever happened to me that I was able to live out one of my biggest and strongest desires. God was working in my life even then, although I really wasn't aware of it at the time. Moving to the beach was the best thing that I could do, and the best place that I could be so that I could begin the healing process. My life was actually beginning when I was so sure that it was ending!

God is our refuge and strength, a very present help in trouble. Psalms 46:1

The cocoon

As I cuddle away from the muddle,
It is best for me to rest,
As I heal from this ordeal.

The bus ride from Salisbury to Myrtle Beach took around six and a half hours. There were layovers in Charlotte and Columbia as well as other stops along the way.

During the long ride, I could not wait to get to Myrtle Beach so that I could begin my new life. I was excited, nervous, and scared. I had never done anything like this before and deep down I was not sure that I could make it on my own. Allan had told me that I would never make it without him and for a long time I had believed that. I later learned this is a tactic abusers use to hold onto their victims.

When I actually arrived at the beach, I was happy to finally be there. I took a cab to the Myrtle Beach Police Department and then an officer drove me to the shelter. I felt so self-conscious riding in the back of the police car that I tried to hide my face. I guess I was afraid people would think I was in trouble or something.

Once at the shelter, I met Camilla, one of the house ladies. She was the only one there.

It was a Tuesday evening and all the women who stayed there had gone to a weekly meeting at a local church for counseling. Camilla was nice and she helped me to get settled in. By then I was starting to feel a little homesick. Also I was beginning to worry about how I would get around without a car, where I would find a job, and where I would live eventually. Camilla taught me about doing things in "baby steps." That little bit of advice has been very helpful to me at other times in my life.

I met some of the other women when they got back from counseling, as well as my roommate. It took a while for me to get used to things at the shelter. The next day was July 4th and I missed being with family. We usually got together to celebrate it.

July 6th started out like any other day. We got up, did our assigned chores, and later that morning I went to DSS with some of the women to see what kind of help we could get. On the way back to the house, I noticed the humidity in the air seemed so thick that I could hardly breathe and that afternoon the strand was hit with a terrible storm!

I have always been a person to run to the windows every few minutes during a storm.

They have always frightened me. When I went to the kitchen window and looked out, I could not believe what I was seeing. I was looking at a tornado! It was a grey funnel shape at the top and the sky was an icky grey-green. I watched it a second or two and asked someone "Is that what I think it is?" I was trying to stay calm as I did not want to cause panic, but looking at that swirling thing was scary! It looked as though it was coming toward the house! Let me tell you, I never want to see a sight like that again! That was definitely one of the scariest moments of my life! The house mothers, as we sometimes called them, made us get into the hallway and we had to stay there until the danger passed.

For the rest of the day I could not believe that I had actually been in a tornado and I felt so sick that I could not eat. It was a miracle that nobody had been seriously hurt. For a while after that, my best friend Amelia nicknamed me weather girl. When I talked to my cousin later, he asked me if I was okay and did I still want to live there after being in that and I said yes. He had heard about the tornado and was concerned about me.

During the following weeks, women came and went. We were required to attend the weekly counseling sessions. I would get counseling at the shelter too. When I first met Penny, one of my counselors, I liked her right away. There was something about her that reminded me of one of my cousins on the Watson side. She was easy to talk to and she helped me with the issues that I needed to deal with. I learned so much from her!

I often thought I did something to cause the abuse, or that maybe I deserved it. I now know that is not true. I did not cause it, I did not want it, and I did not deserve it! With the abuser, it is always about control. There were times when I did fight back and Allan did not like that.

Although I was where I had always wanted to be, I still had a tough time dealing with the things my husband had done to me. I was trying my best to move on, but it was not easy. Scars heal, but hurtful words never completely go away. Penny once told me that it can take up to 40 positive comments to override just one negative comment.

I made several good friends at the shelter and we did what we could to help each other. A few times Sidney, the main day-time house-mother, let me go with her to run errands or pick up donations and I enjoyed that. My best friend Amelia had five children. They were sweet kids and such a joy to be around. Sometimes at night we gathered in their room and read some in my book before bed. They were fascinated that I was writing a novel and they loved the story.

Amelia, the children, and I went to the beach whenever we could and we always had fun. The ocean was only a few blocks from where we lived and most of the time we walked. One day when we were on the way to the beach, we met an elderly lady who happened to be out in her front yard. She needed help with something so we stopped and did what we could for her.

Maggie became a good friend and not long after we met, she called me. She needed someone to help clean up at her house. She had been sick and was unable to do some of the things herself. Maggie paid me for cleaning up the kitchen, which had been a terrible mess, and later that afternoon one of her friends came to visit. The lady was so impressed with the job that I had done that she paid me too, even though she did not know me! It was such a great blessing, and it was nice being able to get out and help someone who really needed it.

Most days I stayed in at the shelter. It was too hot to go out and walk far. I learned that the hard way when I had been out walking with friends and ended up fainting. It took a while for me to get used to the hot weather in South Carolina. Compared to where I had grown up in North Carolina, it could be much hotter. Summertime is not one of my favorite times of the year. That seems to be when some of my health issues flare up the most and I don't like to be outside much because of my allergies.

One day I became very sick and ended up having to go to the hospital by ambulance. I had a bad case of bronchitis and I felt awful! I did not think I was ever going to get back to the shelter. I called a few times trying to get a way back. Only a few women who stayed at the shelter had a car and it seemed like I had to wait forever to be picked up. Eventually, one of the ladies who volunteered at the shelter did come to get me.

When I finally did get back home, one of my roommates had a nice surprise waiting for me. There were several stuffed rabbits on my bed that had not been there when I left out that morning. The shelter had gotten in a donation of toys. My roommates knew how much I loved rabbits and that gesture of kindness meant so much to me! I did not keep all of the rabbits though. I gave them back for the children who came to the shelter.

A few days later, I had to go back to the hospital. I had a red rash on my back and it itched so badly! My friends weren't sure what it was and one lady said it looked like shingles. That really frightened me! The weekend house-mother drove me to the hospital in Conway to have it checked out. I have no idea why she took me way up there.

I do not remember for sure what I had, but the medicine the doctor prescribed must have helped. The rash and itch got better; however, the meds I was on for that made me very sick on my stomach. I could not eat much for several days, but eventually I did feel better.

In mid-August, Amelia and the children found a house nearby and they moved out of the shelter. It hurt to see them go and leaving was hard on the children too. We all had become very close.

A couple weeks later, Lorna came down for a visit with two of her friends. She was the same girl who had met Bobby and Rikki with me a few weeks earlier at the Poison concert. Lorna, her friends, and I went out to eat at the Hard Rock Café, and then we went shopping at Broadway at the Beach. Lorna and I were both wearing the same Poison tee shirt that day and that was not planned!

I really wanted out of the shelter, but I still did not have a car or a job yet. It was very hard getting around the strand without a car and it was even harder trying to find a way to get somewhere.

Geraldine, another counselor who also worked with me, arranged for me to meet with a man from the vocational workshop. I worked there for about two weeks but soon discovered it was not for me. It was located in Conway and I rode in a van with a few other people to get there and back. I had a hard time with some of the things there and I ended up quitting. I knew I could eventually get something better in Myrtle Beach.

Geraldine was not happy that I had left the workshop. I did not like disappointing her, but around that time I was having migraine headaches. Some days I just wanted to be left alone. I really needed to go to a chiropractor for treatment, but I had not found one yet.

One day when I was feeling well enough to venture out and it was not too hot, I went for a walk near the Pavilion. I needed time to be by myself to think and I was listening to a Poison tape on my headset. While I was walking around, I started to wonder whether or not I really wanted to be there. I loved the beach and I had always wanted to live there, but it was so hard being there without a way to support myself that I felt like giving up.

As I was listening to the song Cry Tough, I realized I did not want to leave yet and give up on my dreams. Life does get hard at times but you can't just quit when it gets tough. Once again, I was finding strength in a song that I loved, by the band that I loved.

Soon after that, I began to look for a job that would be close enough to walk. At first I was not sure where to go, as there were quite a few small businesses in that area, but when I went into the dry cleaners, I talked to a man and he told me to check back the next day. When I went back, I talked to his brother and I was hired!

I was so happy and relieved to have finally found work, and I had gotten the job without anyone helping me! I started the new job on the Friday before Labor Day weekend. I put the plastic bags over the clothes, stapled the tag to the bag, and sent them down the line to go out. It was hot, tiring work, but it was enjoyable. All during that weekend, I was bored and could hardly wait to go back to work on Tuesday.

After I had worked for a few days, I noticed a chiropractor two doors down from the cleaners. I went in and talked to the man and he was nice. I started going to him for treatment. The best part of all was that he gave a discount to women who had been in the shelter, and his treatment also included massage therapy, at no extra charge. It was truly a blessing finding a chiropractor that close! It is so amazing how God can work things out like that!

I liked working at the cleaners and most of all I liked having a job where I was close enough to walk. Most of my coworkers seemed nice. One of the ladies who worked close to me knew a little about what I had been through. She talked to me about having confidence, and with her advice I began to say "I can do this!" whenever I was faced with something I didn't think I could do. Even now, I still think of her whenever I'm struggling to do something that is hard.

I met another lady who came to the shelter with her little girl. We became friends and she took me to a few places. One evening we went to a resort hotel and rode on the lazy river inside. It was fun but I was concerned about getting caught. Somehow her oldest daughter had gotten us in.

During my time in the shelter, I met and talked to women who went through abuse fifteen, twenty, even thirty years! I am so thankful that I got out when I did. I realize now it wasn't that hard for me to leave Allan because I did not love him and it was a relief finally being away from the abuse.

Most women truly do love the man that they are with, but they will only leave when they are good and ready. Quite a few women ended up going back to that kind of life because of fear of the unknown. I watched it happen over and over. I made my mind up then and there, that was not going to be me!

I can do all things through Christ which strengtheneth me. Philippians 4:13

The Butterfly

And now I soar out the door,
To go high up to the sky.
Then got the notion,
To land at the ocean.

After I had worked for a while, I was ready to find a place to live. I had been at the shelter for over two months and it was time to move on. One evening when I was out walking with another lady, I looked for a place and I even checked at motels.

The place I found was quite run-down, but it was the best that I could do. It was close enough to work that I could walk, and I made enough that I could pay the weekly rate. I thought it over for a couple days and then I decided that I would take it.

I moved in on a Saturday. Another lady who was staying at the shelter at that time had a car and she helped me move. I was so grateful and so excited that I finally had a place of my own, and I absolutely loved my motel room. It had a king size bed and a small kitchen. I was able to make my room look nice with a few things that I had gotten at the shelter from donations. What I liked the most was being able to see the ocean from the balcony. The beach was across the boulevard from my new home!

I was finally independent and it was exciting. At the same time it was very scary too. It was the first time in my life that I had ever lived alone! It was something I never thought I could do, but with God's help I was doing it! It took some time to get used to living alone.

Although I lived alone, I wasn't alone. I still went to Penny for counseling every week at the shelter. I worked at the dry cleaners Monday through Friday, and I talked to mom on the phone when I could.

I became friends with some of the people at the motel, and one Friday night several of us sat near the messed up pool talking. It had been badly damaged in the tornado that had hit the strand that summer. I really enjoyed being out there with other people, and it was nice not being cooped up in my room.

It was about a ten minute walk between the cleaners and the motel. Every day when I walked home from work, I could see the ocean from a hill on the avenue, and I thanked God for letting me live so close to the beach. I was healing and growing, and venturing out more. Late one afternoon, I walked to Kmart and bought a small CD player for my room.

I had not been out of the shelter long when someone donated a bike for me. It was a man's big bike and I was afraid of it when I first saw it. I had not ridden a bike in years, but I accepted it anyway. I slowly got used to riding it and I was allowed to keep it inside during work hours.

One day, when I had gotten caught up and was waiting on orders to be sent down my line to be bagged, I was gazing out the window. A man was riding his bike when suddenly; a van hit him from behind and knocked him off! I could not believe what I had just witnessed and I started screaming. It did not take my coworkers long to figure out something had happened. I think some of them tried to calm me down, but I really don't remember. I was in too much shock.

One thing is for sure; an angel must have caught that man! He was eventually okay and he still rode a bike after what had happened to him! I found out that two of his nieces worked at the same place I did and I often asked about him. They always said, "Yeah, he's still riding!" He was a very blessed and brave man for sure; however, just seeing that accident had scared me so badly that I would not go near my bike.

After a few weeks, I did get my courage up and I rode my bike around in a vacant parking lot beside the motel. Denny, the maintenance man got my bike out for me every morning before I went to work. He kept it locked up at night and put air in the tires when they needed it. I lived on the second floor so there was no way that I could keep the bike up in my room.

I liked talking to Denny and he became one of my best friends. I always enjoyed hanging out with him even though he was much older than me. He liked to drink beer and smoke pot, but he had a heart of gold. He looked after me when I lived at the motel and I was thankful that he became a part of my life. When I had first moved to the motel, I did not realize he worked there and I had ignored him when he spoke to me. Being on my own for the first time in my life, I was afraid of everyone and trusted no one.

One Sunday evening, Denny and I walked along the boulevard and we looked for a place that had ice cream. Most of the places like that had closed for the season, but we did eventually find a place that still served it.

Denny was a kind and generous man, and one night he gave me and another girl, who also lived at the motel, some money so that we could play putt-putt at a nearby course. We had a lot of fun and I greatly appreciated his kindness.

A few weeks later, it was fall bikers week in Myrtle Beach and a lot of bikers stayed at our motel. Denny and I talked to some of them and I met one from Salisbury who actually knew one of my cousins! One of the bikers took me for a ride on the boulevard. I had never been on a motorcycle before and it was awesome! It was fun having bikers stay at the motel, but it was extremely noisy! They would be out riding on the boulevard until like two or three in the morning and sleep was impossible.

I had not been back to North Carolina at all since I had moved to the beach on July 3rd. It was now mid-October and my mother was getting married. The day before the wedding, my uncle and cousin drove down to South Carolina to get me and I gave them money for gas.

I was not able to be with mom until the next day when my cousin drove me to the church to meet everyone. I was going to be the maid of honor for my mother, and I had to borrow a dress from my cousin because I did not have anything suitable to wear. My emotions were everywhere. I felt happy, sad, and excited, all at the same time.

A major change was getting ready to take place. I would be getting a dad, two brothers, a sister, and nieces and nephews. As an only child, I had always wanted brothers and sisters, and at twenty-nine years old, it was finally happening. I liked Lynne and Dale right away when I met them, but the older brother had not been able to come.

The wedding was beautiful and my sister sang a song in it. I cried through most of it. Then later we all went out for lunch at a restaurant in town. It was so much fun being around relatives that I had not seen in a while and meeting my new family.

I wasn't sure what I wanted to do. I had siblings now, but they all lived in North Carolina and I lived in South Carolina. It would be hard to spend time together. I was living out my dream of living in South Carolina and I was independent. I had a job, a home, (even though it was in a motel) and a car again. I was not ready to leave the beach yet and the final decision was to go back.

I would be getting the car that mom helped me to get a few months before I met

Allan. It was a teal green 1993 Oldsmobile Achieva and I was very happy to get it back! I had left it for her when she sold her car, but she didn't need it anymore. Her new husband had a car and a truck.

After lunch, we went to mom's apartment and I packed up a lot of my stuff to take back with me. Early the next morning, after spending the second night at my aunt, uncle, and cousin's house, I left to go back to South Carolina. I was very nervous about making that long trip by myself, and I stopped only once to get gas.

When I got home, it took a while for me to figure out where to put everything. I had so much stuff that I donated some of it to the shelter. Later that week, mom and Rob came to visit me. They did not like where I was at.

On Halloween night, I went out to eat with Amelia and her family, and after supper we took the kids trick or treating. It was so much fun running around with them. I had not seen them in a while and it was great to catch up. She had ended up going back to her husband and I was concerned. He was mean and he argued with her a lot.

A few nights later, I went to the House of Blues for the Alice Cooper concert. I had bought my ticket a couple weeks earlier. I liked some his songs and I really wanted to see him in concert. It was a very interesting show, and it was so nice to be able to go out and do something like that by myself. Allan used to tell me that I could not do things on my own, and one of the reasons I went to the concert by myself was to prove to myself that I could!

When I got back to the motel that night, Brewster, another good friend, came over and we hung out most the night talking. He was a fun person to be around and he could make me laugh. Another time when he came to visit, I was embarrassed because I had my underwear hanging up to dry. I had tied a piece of string to the lamps above each side of the bed to use for a short clothesline.

By working at the cleaners, I was allowed to have ten articles of clothing washed for free each week, but I washed my other stuff by hand in the bathroom sink. It was not the easiest thing to do, but I figured it was cheaper than taking them to a laundromat.

A few weeks later, I moved to a room on the back side of the motel. Denny had been doing some renovations and I got a room he had already worked in. Soon he would be working on the side where I had lived and I would have to move eventually anyway. He did awesome woodwork, but I did not like this room. It was smaller and did not have a kitchen. I could no longer see the beach.

The day before Thanksgiving, I drove up to North Carolina after work. Mom and Rob met me at Kmart because I was not sure how to get to their trailer and I would be staying with them. They had the meal and it was nice seeing my new siblings and their families. I also met my oldest brother Eugene and his wife Kris for the first time. I enjoyed talking to them and getting to know them better.

When I got back to South Carolina on Saturday, I was upset to find out that Denny had moved out of the motel. Something had happened while I had been away, but I'm not sure what. I went to my room and cried for a long time. I was also missing my family.

That night, I went out with Brewster and Leila, another friend who lived in another motel nearby. He called a cab and we went to a club to hear some beach music. It was a nice distraction for a while, but when I got home I cried all over again.

Sometime that week, I moved out of the motel and moved into another one across the street. It was a block further from the ocean, but in some ways I liked it better. I had more room, I was on the ground floor, and I was able to hook up my computer to use the internet. Brewster lived and worked there, and he helped me with things when I needed it. However, I did not live there long.

I do not remember why I moved so soon, but this time I went to another motel on the boulevard further down the strand. It was the nicest place of all, with two beds and a kitchen. I found out Denny was living and working two motels away and I often walked over to visit him.

One weekend, mom and Rob came down to see me. I had a chest cold and they took me to Walgreens to get some medicine. I felt better after a few days. During the time I lived at that Inn, I started attending a Lutheran church and I really liked it.

I did not drive to North Carolina for Christmas and it was hard being away from my family during the holidays. On Christmas Eve, Denny brought me some cheese and crackers, and Penny invited me to a dinner at the shelter on Christmas day. It was nice being around other ladies. I was not alone at New Year's Eve either. Maggie invited me to spend the night with her and that's what I did. We watched TV and enjoyed each other's company.

The new year brought a lot of changes, both good and bad. In late January I moved again. Another guy that I knew from the second motel where I had stayed helped me to find an apartment. We had talked and hung out a few times, but we did not stay friends. He wanted us to be more than friends and I was not ready for that. When I told him how I felt, he got upset and did not want to be friends at all. It hurt being treated that way, but I did not need someone like him.

Penny had a hard time keeping up with me because I moved around so much, but I continued my counseling with her. I was tired of living in motels and I wanted to do better, but I did not like the apartment either. It was small with only one bedroom and it smelled like an old basement. That's not a good thing if you have allergies and asthma as I do. I tried not to be there any more than I had to be, and some nights I stayed with Amelia's family.

Sometime in February, mom and Rob came down to see the apartment. They did not like it much either. We found out about an apartment complex that Penny thought would be a good place for me to live and we went to see about it. Right away I liked the lady who was the landlord and I decided I wanted to live there.

We were blessed to find this place when we did. The next day, I was laid off from my job at the cleaners. I worried about what would happen now, but God worked it out. The rent on those apartments was based on income, and since I was not working, I would not have to pay rent until I went back to work. I was able to move in right away and that was truly a blessing! Mom and Rob helped me move, and we went to a used furniture store to get a couch. It was a sleeper sofa and I used it until I got a bed.

My new home was in Socastee, about twenty minutes from the beach, but I liked my new apartment. However, within a few weeks I felt bored. I did not know anyone and I had not found a job yet. It was nice not having to worry about rent and the car was paid off, but I had other bills.

Not long before Allan and I separated, I made the mistake of taking out a cash advance on a credit card. I did not know the interest would be so high! If I could have known my marriage would be over soon, I never would have taken out that money! Now, I was stuck having to pay it all back by myself and I worried about it a lot.

Mom and Rob soon came down again and they bought a mattress. When we went to a consignment store, they bought a bed frame and a big beautiful painting of a beach scene for me. Amelia gave me a glass top kitchen table with two chairs and I was really glad to get those things.

That spring, I finally got a job at a shoe store in Surfside. I liked the ladies that I worked with, but I had never cared for retail. I made the best of it anyway. It was the first time that I had ever operated a cash register, and it was nice learning something different.

I did eventually meet my next door neighbor, a guy around my age. We hung out a few times, but he was not someone that I enjoyed being around. Like so many guys that I had met, he had a bad attitude.

A few weeks later, I got a nice surprise. When mom and Rob came down for a visit, they brought my sister Lynne, and we had so much fun together! We all went to Huntington Beach State Park. We played on the beach, walked around, and explored

Atalaya, the big castle there. We took pictures and enjoyed being together.

One night while they were there, we went out to eat at an awesome seafood restaurant in Garden City. The food was delicious, but boy I thought my step-dad was going to have a cow when he found out the price. It was over $90 for all four of us!

In May, I went to two great concerts. The Chairmen of the Board performed at the House of Blues and I went to see them. They had always been my favorite beach band and it was neat getting to see them at the beach.

The next weekend, Lorna, another girl, and I traveled to Valdosta, Georgia to see Poison and Cinderella in concert and I was so excited! We spent the day riding rides at the amusement park and that night we watched the show. I was ecstatic to see the band again, but I was upset because Lorna had not gotten a ticket for me to be in the seating section with them. I did not understand that at all; she knew I was going and she should have gotten one for me too. After the concert, it was pouring down rain and I had to wait for them to find me. Back then I did not own a cell phone. I was glad when I finally got back home the next day.

For my 30'th birthday, mom and Rob came to be with me. I had to work that day and my coworkers gave me a card and a balloon. That evening, mom and Rob took me out to eat at a seafood restaurant up in Calabash, North Carolina and it was good. I enjoyed my birthday. Lynne called me and Amelia called me too. I was off the next day and we went to Brookgreen Gardens. It was very beautiful, and I admired the flowers and the statues.

The next day was not as good though. I had gotten an infection and I was in so much pain. I had to get medicine and it took a while to clear up.

On July 3'rd, I had lived in South Carolina exactly one year and something unexpected happened to me that day too; I met Roger. I went to spend the day with Amelia and the children and he was sitting on the couch. I did not think about him much at first and I played outside with the kids in a small pool for a while.

When we went in later, I asked Amelia about him. Roger was one of her husband's friends and when we met, we seemed to like each other right away. He was Cherokee Indian and he was gorgeous. We went to see one of his friends and she warned me to be careful. It was too late; I was already falling for him.

That evening we went to the Garden City pier to see a live band and later we sat on the beach and talked for a long time. I had promised Amelia's kids that I would spend the night with them and although it was very late, we went to my apartment to get a few things. The kids were already in bed when we got back, but Roger and I still stayed overnight anyway.

The next day we were with them for a while. Roger and I had to go to the store and the kids wanted to go with us. We let them ride along. My car did not have AC and they were hot and complaining.

When we were hanging out in a gazebo at a church near their house, the kids gave me flowers. They seemed to like Roger too and they said we were cute together. I felt so happy being there with them and Roger that day! That was the first time that I had ever felt romance with a guy and I really thought he was the one.

Later that afternoon, Roger and I went to see Maggie. I was getting a migraine and starting to feel sick. I was supposed to work that evening but I didn't know if I could. Roger took me to the store and bought me the medicine that I needed. I do not remember if I called in or if I went in anyway. It was July 4th and I didn't want them to think I was staying out because of the holiday.

I did work the next evening. Roger took me and then he picked me up. After work we drove along Ocean Boulevard for a while. When I told him about the Poison concert that would be in Virginia Beach Sunday night, we decided that we would go and we left out Saturday evening. We stopped at Amelia's first and hung out, and then later we were on the way. I drove up most of the way and it took several hours.

Late that night, we stopped and spent the night with Roger's cousin and his wife, who lived in Richmond. They seemed like nice people and we were with them for a few hours. We left soon after lunch.

It took a couple more hours to get to Virginia Beach, and I was so happy when we finally got there! We found a small motel and when I was telling the man that we were there for the Poison concert, he handed me two tickets for the lawn! I could hardly believe it, but that was an awesome blessing!

The man just gave us the Poison concert tickets for staying at his motel! I had not ordered tickets because I did not know that we would be going. God sure does have an awesome way of working things out!

Roger and I went to the beach and explored the strand until it was time to drive to the amphitheater. It was about ten miles from the beach. We missed most of the Cinderella concert, but I was so happy to see Poison perform in Virginia Beach!

The next morning we drove back to Myrtle Beach and a day or two after that, Roger and I broke up. He had stayed with me for a week, but he liked to drink. He had not touched a drop at all that I knew of while we were in Virginia, but sooner or later I knew it would be an issue. His drinking was the only thing we ever argued about and I kicked him out because I could not handle it.

It was so hard and so painful going through that! I had grown to really care about Roger and it hurt letting him go. We had so much fun together and he was the only man who had ever made me feel special. He had a good heart and he bought me a few things that I needed. I know he cared about me, but he cared about drinking more.

As I tried to get over Roger, I spent time with Amelia and the children. Having them in my life helped me so much that I wanted to help them too. One afternoon the kids were so hungry that they were crying. Their sorry daddy would not go to the store and get them food. Amelia was so stressed out about things in her life that I offered to keep the girls overnight, and then I took them to my apartment and cooked supper for them.

I get angry when I see men being mean to women or children. One time when I was at the pier with my mom and step-dad, I heard a man putting down his wife or girlfriend, and cussing her out while they were fishing. It made me so mad that I wanted to smack his head off! I felt helpless because I wanted to do something to help, but I couldn't.

During the weeks after I broke up with Roger, I was so upset and stressed out that it started to affect my health. Late one afternoon, I was on my way to work when I suddenly started feeling numb or tingly on my left side. Having those feelings frightened me, and I pulled off at the nearest place I saw, which happened to be a fire department. I told the men who came out how I was feeling and I was taken to Conway hospital in an ambulance. I did not know what was happening to me and I was really scared!

I don't remember what the doctor at the hospital said or what they did. They didn't tell me much of anything, and when I was released I called Sarah, a new friend who I had met through Amelia recently. She came to get me and we got my car later.

I had to quit my job at the shoe store, and mom and Rob came down to be with me because I was ill. She called our doctor in North Carolina and got an appointment for me to go to him. Penny told me that my scary experience had probably been a very bad panic attack. She said they can do all kinds of strange things to a person, even make them feel as though they are dying.

During this time, I found out more bad news. Amelia and her family would be moving away from the beach. I would miss them so much and I was very upset. It seemed as though everything, and then some, was going wrong in my life.

A few days later, I followed mom and Rob back to North Carolina and I decided to stay for a couple weeks. I went to my doctor and I began to feel better. I rested when I could and I visited relatives. One evening, my aunts, uncles, and cousins came over to mom and Rob's mobile home, and we all had dinner together. It was great being able to see every one again.

When I returned home to South Carolina two weeks later, I had a horrible mess in my refrigerator. Everything had spoiled and it smelled awful! I got the stuff out as quickly as I could and carried the smelly stuff to the dumpster. Then I cleaned up the refrigerator the best I could. Sarah took me to the grocery store and bought a few things for me, and I was so grateful!

Later that week, I drove to Fayetteville, North Carolina for another Poison concert. It was around a two and a half hour drive and it was raining. I was supposed to meet Lorna and another girl at the coliseum, but they were late getting there. I had to stay outside and wait for them so that I could give their tickets to them. We had ordered them earlier in the summer. I missed seeing the opening band perform and I was not happy.

Poison was scheduled to perform the next night at the House of Blues in Myrtle Beach, and we said we were going. I waited all day for Lorna to let me know about that show, but she never called or came by. (I did hear from her weeks later and that was the last time we ever spoke.) I never knew if she had tickets for that concert or not, but I know it's my fault for not getting my own tickets. I should have ordered them and went by myself. Sometimes it's better that way than dealing with people you can't trust.

That night I went over to Sarah's and I cried a lot. I felt so much sadness, anger, and hurt that I did not know what to do! She helped me to feel some better and after talking and thinking things over, I decided what I was going to do.

At the Fayetteville concert, it had been announced that the fans who attended that show could bring their ticket stub to the Charlotte show on Saturday and get in free. I had the chance to go to another Poison concert for free and I was going to take it! 2002 is the only year that I ever remember them doing that.

I left Saturday morning and drove up to North Carolina. I spent a few hours with Lynne and then I drove to Charlotte that evening. It was nice not having to worry about waiting on other people, and I was able to see all the bands perform. When it started to rain, it felt so refreshing that I raised my arms up in thanksgiving and let it fall on me. (The free ticket was for the lawn, which meant I had plenty of freedom to move.)

I had been to four Poison concerts that year, and that seemed to be the best show of them all. It was exactly what I needed to work through my anger, pain, and frustration. Rock concerts have always been a positive outlet for me. I was feeling better physically, mentally, and emotionally, and I was also feeling something else that I had not felt in such a long time; joy! God had provided a way for me to overcome some deep hurts and disappointments, through seeing my favorite band in concert again, and I was thanking him for those showers of blessings!

I stayed in North Carolina all week so that I could attend a family reunion on Sunday. It was nice visiting with relatives that I had not seen in a long time. After the reunion, I drove back to South Carolina and on the way home I was caught in a storm. It was scary driving in that much rain for over two hours.

In September, I got a job cleaning at some businesses in the evenings. Most of the time I worked with a few other people, but one place I was assigned to clean by myself on certain nights. It was a huge building, but I got it done. Sometimes during the day, we would go in and clean houses that had been built recently. It wasn't long though until I was laid off from that cleaning company. For a while I did what few odd jobs I could find, but it was much harder finding work at the beach in the fall.

A few weeks later, I got sick. I'm not sure what I had, but I was achy and I felt awful. I was sick on my stomach too. It scared me because I never had it that bad and I didn't know what to do! That was one time when it was frightening being on my own. Whatever I had finally went away after several days and I felt better, but it sure had been rough!

On Halloween, mom and Rob came to visit me after they had been to Hilton Head for their 1 year anniversary. I always enjoyed it when they came. Sarah called me the next day. She needed me to take her daughter Suzanne to pick up her grandson. It was their weekend to get him. I didn't want to leave mom and Rob, but they were okay with it. I would only be gone for a few hours. I drove Suzanne to Pelion to pick up her son from her ex-husband. It was a nice trip and we talked a lot, but I was so glad when I got back home late that night.

About a week later, I drove Suzanne and her boyfriend Timmy to Laurinburg to get one of his friends. They had wanted me to meet him, and I guess they had hoped we would like each other. The guy was not my type and also he was not an easy person to get along with. One night we were having an argument about something and Sarah's big reddish-brown dog started barking at us. It was embarrassing and I was glad when the guy finally went back home soon after Thanksgiving.

That year, I ate with Sarah and her family. They had moved to their new house in Myrtle Beach a few weeks before. I spent a lot of time with them and they often took me out to eat at Ryan's. Sarah was a great friend and she helped me with things when I needed it. Her daughter liked to write stories and I let her read the novel I was writing.

One afternoon when I was leaving their house, I totaled my car. God was watching out for me in that situation! It so happened that Suzanne's boyfriend decided to follow me home and I was really thankful he did. A rod had blown through the motor and the car died in the middle of the road. Timmy had been keeping check on my car because I had been having problems with it for a while, and I think he knew something was getting ready to happen to it. It had cut off on me one night when I was taking someone home a few weeks earlier.

The car had to be towed somewhere and Sarah took me wherever I needed to go. I had a big problem trying to get the title so that I could do something with the car, and it was upsetting and frustrating. Mom and Rob came down several days before Christmas to get me and we finally got that mess straightened out.

I spent Christmas with my family and relatives. I enjoyed it as much as I could but I could not help worrying about not having a car anymore. Mom and Rob took me back to South Carolina a few days later and I really missed them. I don't remember how I got there, but I spent New Year's Eve with Brewster, Denny, and his roommate Sharon at the motel. We had a lot of fun just hanging out and I was grateful to be with good friends and not home alone.

January was cold and boring. I was unable to go anywhere unless someone took me. It was hard being without a car again, and it was too cold and too far to walk anywhere.

One weekend, Roger came to visit me when his son brought him over to stay for a few days. It was good to see him again and we talked about a lot of things. I had said some mean things to him when we broke up and I had felt bad about hurting him. Roger told me that he had cared about me as much as I had cared for him. It was comforting hearing that, but deep down I knew things could never work out between us. It was hard when he left, but I was grateful we had the time to talk. He had decided to get help for his drinking.

In early February, I was blessed with a car. My landlord, who was also a pastor at a local church, was able to help me get it. I had attended her church a few times when she took me and she was a very nice lady.

One of the deacons from church worked at a car place and he helped me get the car there. I was so thankful for their help that I continued to attend their church; not out of obligation, but because I really liked it. It was a lot closer than the Lutheran church and I liked the people.

I began job hunting, and I drove up to North Carolina to be with mom for her birthday in March. Soon after I got back home, a man from another cleaning company called me and I got that job. I was happy to have a job again and I liked the people that I worked with.

During the week we traveled to different places near the beach, such as Pawley's Island or North Myrtle Beach and we mostly did residential cleaning. I did not like cleaning other peoples' houses. Some of the cleaning stuff bothered my allergies and I was always afraid I would break something.

A few weeks later, Lynne called and told me that mom was in the hospital. I quickly packed a few things and left. It was at night, but I got up to Lynne's house in Salisbury as soon as I possibly could. I was scared and worried, and we didn't know what was going to happen.

Mom came home from the hospital a few days later, and during that time I had decided I was ready to move back to North Carolina. Her cousin Kathleen offered to let me move in with her. Sabina drove me to her home in Cleveland to see it and I accepted her offer.

Sabina and I drove back to the beach that night. We packed my stuff and rented a truck the next day. I spent time saying goodbye to my friends. I was sad about leaving them and the beach, but I realized my heart just wasn't there anymore. It was time to go home.

I lived in Myrtle Beach for twenty-one months and I experienced some awesome and not so awesome things. I've seen a car chase and a tornado, but no matter what I went through, I was determined that I was not going to be a fallen angel. Yes, that is a Poison song, from the soundtrack of my life. I cannot tell you how many people made the comment to me; they can't imagine someone as quiet as I am going to rock concerts!

I was excited about starting over in North Carolina. Mom did eventually recover from whatever had made her very sick. The doctor thought she had lung cancer, but when they did testing on her later, they could not find anything at all! God is so good!

I really liked staying with Kathleen. Her husband was a truck driver and he was often on runs across the country. After I had been there a few weeks, she helped me to get a job at a nursing home in town. I enjoyed working there and I liked some of my coworkers. I stayed busy that summer and some days before I went to work, I stayed with my niece and nephew while Lynne took classes at the community college.

In October, I saw a lawyer about getting a divorce. I was worried that I would have to stay married because I didn't know where to find Allan. We had not talked in over two years, and I had to have an ad put in the paper in the last known area where he had lived. If he didn't show up to contest the divorce, I would be able to get it in a few months. I could not get it soon enough!

One morning I woke up with pain in my right side. I thought it was just a catch from the way I had slept and I went about my day as usual. I was off and I did some errands. That night the pain became very bad and mom prayed over me. She took me to the doctor the next morning with Rob and I couldn't help feeling scared. The doctor examined me and over the next few days I had tests done at the hospital.

During one of the scans I had to lie on a table and be still for about an hour, and then they gave me some stuff to drink. After that, I had to lie still for another hour while they did another scan, and I started to hurt. I watched an image on a screen nearby, but I had no idea what it meant. I just knew something was wrong to be in that much pain and all I did was drink something.

The test results revealed that my gall bladder was not functioning properly; it would have to come out. Looking back, I realize that many of the times that I had been sick in South Carolina may have been from that all along, but at the time I didn't know what it was. There had been a time when my chiropractor had suspected a problem with my gall bladder, but it had gotten better, or so I thought.

I applied for financial aid and thankfully I was able to get it through vocational rehab. I had surgery in November, right before Thanksgiving. It was the worst pain that I had ever experienced, but after the healing process I felt much better. When I went back at work, one of my coworkers commented that I seemed to have more energy.

Soon after the first of the year, I moved to an apartment in Spencer. I was grateful to have my own place again. I got my divorce in April and I was so happy that I was finally free from Allan. I moved on with my life and I was always hoping to do better for myself.

Later that summer, I left my job at the nursing home to begin work in a department store. I did not like working in retail, but I thought I could earn more money. That was a huge mistake. Money is not everything. I had quit doing something I liked for something I did not like, and I paid for it in more ways than one. I should have stayed at the nursing home until something that really was better came along.

2005 was not a good year. I injured my knee at work and I went through a big mess because of it. I could not stand or walk for long and I really needed to have surgery. A few months later, I quit my job at the store to take care of myself. I tried to do some temporary work, but that did not go well.

In October, my step-dad became sick and passed away suddenly. That was a hard time for all of us. I moved in with mom and I have been with her since. With not working, I could not afford the apartment anyway.

I was finally able to have surgery on my knee about a month later. My knee injury actually turned out to be a blessing in disguise. It put me on the path to finding out some important things about myself.

I did not work for over a year, and I took a free one week course about career planning at Davidson County community College. It was for people who were out of work. I found out about a program that would help me get back to work, and I also got some other counseling too.

I have had learning disabilities since I was a small child. I did not do well in school and it did not take long for me to become bored. In 2009, I was diagnosed with ADHD, or attention deficit hyperactive disorder. I cried because I thought it was something bad. Understanding what I know now, I am not surprised at all that I have it, and I often wonder if my life would have been any different if they had found out I had ADHD when I was a child.

It has never been easy for me to learn to do new things, and I often get mad and frustrated when I don't get it the first few times. I have to stop and say, "I can do this!" Then when I finally do learn to do something new, I'm often surprised to find out how simple it really is. In spite of the difficulties, I like learning to do new things.

During the last ten years, I have worked in various places and have tried many different things. Some of them I was not able to do because of certain health issues. A few years ago when I was working in Lexington, my asthma started flaring up and one day it got so bad that I had to be taken to the hospital by ambulance. It was a very frightening and embarrassing experience! I lost that job because I was allergic to a lot of the things that I worked around.

When I worked in Thomasville a few years later, I mostly liked the work, but the building was very old and dirty. I was sick a lot and I often missed days. I did not understand why God placed me in a place like that. Later on, I realized the skills I had learned there had prepared me for something better. It is always better to wait on God, but it can be very hard.

I worked in distribution on and off for three years, until I was no longer able to work at all due to pain from fibromyalgia. During the last few months when I did work, I struggled with it a lot, but at the time I did not know yet what it was.

I can honestly say that I have learned a few things from my mistakes. A few years ago, I got engaged to a man who I had met online. There were things about him that I really liked, but something just did not feel right. Every time I thought about moving back to South Carolina to be with him, I felt sick. I noticed he was like Allan in some ways and I was having second thoughts.

A very concerned aunt and uncle came to me with some things they had somehow found out about him, and I was really glad that they were looking out for me in that way! I broke up with the man and I felt bad about hurting him, but I did not want to get into another bad marriage. A broken engagement hurts very badly, but another divorce later on would have hurt a whole lot worse!

Yes, I have messed up and I have plenty of regrets, but I am not the only one and will not be the only one. We are all human. In some ways what I have been through has made me a better, stronger person. I choose to learn from my mistakes, and experience has taught me that settling for the first thing that comes along is never good.

Settling has always been where I messed up. I could have had something better if I had waited on God, but when I want something, I want it right now. Waiting has always been extremely hard for me, especially when it seems as though nothing is happening. I am the type of person who likes to see results.

There are times when I still struggle with unforgiveness toward Allan. I don't always understand why God expects me to forgive him, after all the things he had done, but He tells us in the Bible that we have to forgive others so that He can forgive us.

Now and then I still feel angry when I think about things, and other times I can laugh about it; to think that Allan could be so dumb as to think he could actually get away with some of the things that he tried to do!

Sometimes even now I am amazed to look back and realize that one of the worst things that had ever happened to me happened in the middle of being able to live out two of my biggest life dreams, meeting my favorite rock band and moving to the beach and it all happened to me within a month!

I keep believing and trusting God that someday my blessings will come, that I will have true love and happiness, but I have to be patient and wait on Him. Most important of all, keep him first in everything!

Delight thyself also in the Lord; and he shall give thee the desires of thine heart. Commit thy way unto the Lord; trust also in him; and he shall bring it to pass. Psalms 37:4-5

Signs of an Abuser

- Hitting or slapping

- Continually shouting at, cussing, or putting you down

- Threatening to harm you, your family, or your friends

- Harming your pets and animals

- Destroying property

- Constantly telling you what to do, trying to control you

- Keep you from working or going anywhere

- Isolating you from other people

- Taking your money, car keys, or other items

- Demanding sex

About the Author

Since Carol was old enough to read and enjoy books, she always knew she wanted to write her own books someday. As an avid music lover growing up, she has always been creative and she began writing when she was 12 years old. With a passion for 80s music and "hair bands," she enjoys going to rock concerts. The thrill of seeing her favorite bands perform live inspires her writing. Her other interests include gaming, crafting, photography, reading, going to the beach, and spending time with family and friends.

Other Work

Hot Rock and Roll Nights
Metal Hearts
The Unforgettable Ballad

Manufactured by Amazon.ca
Acheson, AB